Discovering & Using Your
Spiritual Gifts

KEN HEMPHILL

Developed by: SAMPSON MINISTRY RESOURCES
Distributed by: LIFEWAY CHRISTIAN RESOURCES OF THE SOUTHERN BAPTIST CONVENTION

1-800-458-2772
7:30 a.m. - 5:30 p.m. CT
Monday - Friday
FAX: 615-251-5933

To Order
↔

0-7673-2251-7

LifeWay Christian Resources
Church Customer Service
127 Ninth Avenue North
Nashville, TN 37234-0113

INTRODUCTION

God created us to know Him, to have fellowship with Him, and to serve Him. Many good books have been written and study materials prepared to help us know God and learn what it means to have a personal, intimate relationship with Him. But not much is available to help us understand how we are to serve Him.

Serving God requires four things:

1. An awareness of what the Bible teaches about service.
2. An understanding of how God equips us for service.
3. A commitment to preparation for service.
4. A dedication to a life of service.

All four things, of course, must come out of prayer and a personal concern for the plan and purpose of God for His people. We must know Him, learn to communicate with Him in prayer, and seek His wisdom for living.

His provision for us includes providing spiritual gifts which, when dedicated to Him, make it possible for us to take important steps toward personal growth and spiritual maturity.

- We discover that we have eternal worth in God's sight and are gifted so that we may play our part in His plan of redemption.
- We learn that He has created each of us with individual differences that uniquely equip us for service.
- We see how our unique gifts fit perfectly alongside the gifts of others in the body of Christ, and that all the gifts working together enable us to carry out His purpose for the church.

We also learn that if we do not discover our spiritual gifts, dedicate them to God, and use them, we hinder the work of the church and remove ourselves from the joyful fulfillment of our special purpose in the kingdom of God.

Discovering and using our spiritual gifts is a priority for every Christian! *Serving God: Discovering & Using Your Spiritual Gifts* is an 8-lesson study designed for use in group settings or for personal study. Its purpose is to motivate participants to serve God by discovering their spiritual gifts and using them to build up the church.

NOTE: Ken Hemphill has written two books on spiritual gifts -- *Mirror, Mirror on the Wall: Discovering Your True Self through Spiritual Gifts* and *Spiritual Gifts: Empowering the New Testament Church.* Both books are available through The Sunday School Board of the Southern Baptist Convention and at Christian bookstores.

TABLE OF CONTENTS

HOW TO USE THIS WORKBOOK

The *Serving God* workbook contains eight lessons that coincide with eight video lessons by Dr. Ken Hemphill. Each workbook lesson contains 1) an outline of the main points of the video lesson, 2) a group discussion guide, 3) a *Looking Ahead* section, and 4) five daily Bible studies that serve as connecting links between the lessons. If you are going through *Serving God* as a private study instead of with a group, be sure to work through the discussion guide on your own. It is a critical component of the study.

Lesson 1

A CHALLENGE TO SERVE

"Things which eye has not seen and ear has not heard, and which have not entered the heart of man, all that God has prepared for those that love Him." For to us God revealed them through the Spirit; for the Spirit searches all things, even the depths of God. 1 Corinthians 2:9-10

KEY THOUGHT

God has an eternal purpose for your life. As you understand this marvelous truth and discover the gifts through which God enables you to accomplish that purpose, you can unleash your God-given potential. You can make a difference in your world. You can serve the living God!

OUTLINE OF VIDEO LESSON

God created you with a purpose. This truth can open up a whole new perspective on the importance of your life and prepare you to join Him in a life of fulfilling service.

1. Through this study, you may expect to accomplish several things:

    1) You will learn that you can make a _____ in the world.
    2) You will understand that you have within you the _____ to impact eternity.
    3) You will understand who you were _____ to be -- the unique *you* within.
    4) You will get a clear _____ of who you are.
    5) You will discover how to tap and utilize the supernatural _____ made available to you by the Holy Spirit, enabling you to serve alongside the Creator of the universe.
    6) You will recognize the gift within you and unleash your God-given _____.

2. Many Christians never really experience the joy of serving the Lord because they say: 1) I am not _____, and 2) I am not _____.

3. An understanding of who you are in God's sight can change negative perceptions from the past that may have stunted your spiritual growth and hindered your ability to serve Him. The cloudy images in your childhood _____ can be changed to give you a clear picture of who you are and what God intends for you to be. Satan uses these images as _____ to be replayed in your mind whenever you see an opportunity to serve God with your life.

4. God's solution is _____ of our sin (1 John 1:9). When God forgives sin, He _____ the tape.

5. The first step in discovering our spiritual gifts is to be absolutely certain that we have a personal _____ with Jesus Christ.

6. The premise of this entire study is that God wants you to know the multiplied blessings of serving Him through the spiritual _____ He has for you.

1. We all can remember some individuals who stand out in our minds as outstanding examples of "faithful servants of the Lord." Write the names of two or three of them in the space below and then discuss as a group the qualities and characteristics that made them special.

    _____

    _____

    _____

2. We know that many Christians never really experience the joy of serving the Lord. We suggest two reasons why people don't serve the Lord: 1) they don't feel _____, and 2) they don't feel _____.

3. There are some definite factors that cause people not to feel worthy or qualified when it comes to accepting a place of responsibility in the church. Discuss as a group what some of these factors might be and write them down.

    _____

    _____

4. *Peter and Jan Thomas and their children moved from a small town in Oklahoma to a large city on the East Coast. They'd been very active in the church they left but somehow felt that because of the move they needed to take a sabbatical for a few months, even after they found a new church home. They felt borderline burned out. After finding a place to live, they immediately began visiting around.*

    They liked a particular church near their home, but it was considerably larger than they were accustomed to. Also, it seemed to be full of volunteer leaders who were gifted, motivated and well-trained. In fact, so well gifted and well-trained the Thomases felt a little uncomfortable! They'd never seen anything like it. The church was reaching people for Christ and seemed to have everything under control. Then one Sunday morning, the pastor gave an impassioned plea for more workers. He issued a challenge that touched them. Peter and Jan Thomas had an interesting discussion over lunch that day.

    What do you think they talked about? Why did the pastor's challenge touch them? What was going through their minds? Discuss as a group.

    _____

    _____

5. One of the benefits of discovering and using our spiritual gifts is a new sense of self-worth. Discuss as a group what you think is the basis for this new self-worth. How do you think a Christian's sense of self-worth should be different from that of a non-Christian?

    _____

    _____

6. We refer in the video lesson to "childhood mirrors" that often have negative effects on us for years to come. Here are some negative messages that, if replayed very often in our minds, can rob us of confidence and personal achievement. Fill these in and expand on the list as a group.

    "I'll be surprised if you ever_____!"

    "I can't believe you_____!"

"You probably won't_____!"

"What makes you think_____?"

"That's well and good but_____!"

Have you ever heard --or said -- anything like this? What's the net effect?

7. Share together how negative messages like these can hinder our service to God?

8. How do the following scripture truths set us free from negative messages that can rob us of the joy of serving God and becoming all He wants us to be?

John 1:12 "...but as many as _____ Him, to them He has given the power to become the _____ of God...."

1 John 1:9 "If we confess our sins, He is faithful and just to _____ our sins and to _____ us from all unrighteousness."

Philippians 4:13 "I _____ ____ all things through _____."

Philippians 3:12-14 "...forgetting what lies _____ and reaching _____...."

Romans 8:28 "...all things work _____ for _____."

Galatians 2:20 "...the life I now live in the flesh I live by the _____ of the Son of God who _____ me and _____ himself for me."

9. Not only has God accepted us and forgiven us, He has empowered us to walk in confidence and achieve His great purpose for our lives.

   • We really can make a _____ in the world!
   • We can _____ eternity!
   • We have the unique privilege of _____ the Creator of the universe!

   Can there really be anything more _____ than this?

10. When we hear a challenge like the one Peter and Jan Thomas heard that Sunday morning, we can choose from a variety of responses. Share together what God wants our response to be and why.

11. *"Eye has not seen and ear has not heard...all that God has _____ for those that _____ Him."* 1 Corinthians 2:10

   The rewards of responding to the challenge to serve God are _____!

PERSONAL APPLICATION

1. Write one thought or insight God has impressed upon you during this lesson.

2. Identify one commitment you are willing to make as a result of this lesson.

3. Write the name of one person -- family member or friend -- with whom you will share each week a thought or insight you have gained from *Serving God.*

PETE RUNNELS, former two-time American League batting champion for the Boston Red Sox, is an example of someone whose life was completely dedicated to serving God.

A devoted husband and father, Pete was also a faithful Christian layman year-round. After a long and successful career in baseball, he planted his life deep in the church because that's where he knew he could make a lasting difference. Whatever job needed to be done, he was sensitive to it. Teaching, witnessing, canvassing, public speaking -- to Pete every job represented a need. And his attitude was "I'm open to it. I'm available. I can't believe I get to do this for the Lord."

Often he could be observed leaving a hospital early in the morning after having spent the night sitting with a patient he barely even knew and who was virtually unknown to the rest of the church. Many times he quietly contributed money, shared wise counsel, and used his influence behind the scenes in ways that would never be recognized. But Pete didn't do things to be seen. He did things because they needed to be done.

His work at Camp Champions, a summer camp he founded in the Texas Hill Country, also reflected his servant spirit. He worked feverishly all summer trying to have a lasting influence on boys and girls, as well as their families. But when camp was over for the year, he was back in his place of responsibility the very next Sunday morning.

Pete Runnels -- a true champion in every area of life -- stepped up to the plate of opportunity and accepted the challenge to serve God with all his heart.

The Bible is filled with examples of men and women who stepped up to the plate when called on to carry out God's purposes. Moses and Joshua were chosen and gifted by God for specific tasks. But there are many more -- Isaiah, Daniel, Nehemiah, Peter, and Paul, to name only a few. God fits the person to the job to be done. And He provides all that is necessary to equip the person for the job.

Is it possible that God is preparing *you* for some special assignment? It may not be a parting of the Red Sea, or the collapse of the Walls of Jericho, but in God's sight it may be just as important. What He is doing today is as eternally significant as what He did back then.

Today, God is calling all of us to a deeper, more personal relationship with Himself and a commitment to discipleship and dedicated service. Our response must be: "Now that I understand, I need to serve." That is the purpose of *Serving God* -- to help us discover and use the gifts He has given us for the benefit of the church.

You may indeed sense that God has something special in mind for you. It was not an accident that He made you just as you are. Now, He wants to show you more. He wants you to know that He will impact the dark world through you. And He has handed you a light.

Next week, the lesson focuses on the Giver of gifts, and we will see that God gives gifts for very good reasons. They help you become the person He created you to be, and even more important, they allow you to be a part of His redemptive activity in the world. May He speak clearly to you in the days and weeks ahead!

DAILY BIBLE STUDIES

During this study in *Serving God,* you will find daily Bible studies to illustrate and supplement the lesson material. These Bible studies can serve to reinforce your awareness that you, like the great Bible characters, were created in God's image. In the biblical account, God clearly uses ordinary people to accomplish His purposes, and He does the same today! Let these studies affirm for you that He is the one who will bring His will to pass. He allows us to play a key role in this incredible drama of life. Like the Lord Jesus, our role is that of a servant -- one who is available for any service required by the Master.

Let these Bible studies be a part of your daily devotional time or an introduction to more thorough study of the subjects you will encounter each week in *Serving God.*

Day 1 - Moses: A Man Convinced of His Limitations
Scripture: Exodus 3:1-15; 4:1-17

Most people, otherwise devoted to God and the church, fail to serve God for one or both of two reasons: They think: 1) "I'm not capable," or 2) "I'm not worthy." Moses is an example of both of these -- and an even better example of what God can do with an ordinary man who becomes willing to accept His assignment and act in faith.

God spoke, and Moses objected. "I'm nobody." "How will I explain what I'm doing?" "I can't speak." "Send somebody else." Sound familiar? Have you used these same excuses when called upon to assume a place of service? Think of a time when this may have happened in your life, and write your thoughts about it here. _____
_____
_____

We know, however, that God does not accept our excuses. Our objections always focus on us -- on ourselves, our limitations, our inabilities. What we must realize is that the work of God depends not on us, but on Him. It is His power that brings His purposes to pass. Our responsibility is to be available, obedient, and ready to serve when He opens an opportunity.

Pray that God will show you that in your life, as in the life of Moses, His strength can be made perfect in your weakness. Write that prayer below, and reread it each day this week.
_____
_____
_____
_____
_____
_____

Day 2 - Joshua: Filling a Big Pair of Shoes
Scripture: Joshua 1:6-9

How can you follow someone like Moses? Many a pastor, Sunday School teacher, business leader or mayor has faced that same question. Everybody loves and respects and honors the ones who went before. Can the new leader possibly fill those big shoes?

Joshua faced just this challenge. But very early, God made sure that Joshua understood that it was not so much a challenge to *lead* as it was a challenge to *serve* -- the same challenge we all face today. Where would this leadership ability come from? With Joshua, leadership would come just as it had come to Moses -- from God Himself.

"...you will lead these people to inherit the land I swore to their forefathers to give them...." (Joshua 1:6)

Do you see what gave Joshua the strength to take up God's challenge? God had already promised the land, and He would deliver on His promise. Joshua's assignment was simply to accept God's gift of responsibility and allow Him to bring about what He had promised.

Can you think of other occasions in the Bible when God called a leader to accomplish something God had already promised? Name one or two:_____

_____

_____

Pray that you, like Joshua, will be given wisdom to let God be God in your life, and to join Him as He fulfills His promises to you and to others through you.

Day 3 - Something Better for Us

Scripture: Hebrews 11:23-30, 39-40

Hebrews 11 is often referred to as God's "Honor Roll of Faith." Named first are familiar heroes -- Abraham, Moses, Joshua, David -- through whom God worked His mighty purposes. But the last portion of the chapter describes another set of heroes, unnamed, unknown and unrecognized. We only know that they *all* were faithful:

"These were all commended for their faith, yet none of them received what had been promised..." (Hebrews 11:39)

Why did they not receive what had been promised? Because *"God had planned something better **for us** so that **only together with us** would they be made perfect."* (Hebrews 11:40)

God had planned something better *for us*! You and I make complete the lives of these Old Testament saints. God gave them gifts that enabled them to do His mighty work, and He has given us gifts for the same purpose today.

Do you see things happening in our world today that indicate that God is working to enlarge and extend the ministry of these faithful people of the Bible? Think it over carefully and write down your thoughts. _____

_____

_____

As you consider God's purpose for your life, pray that you will focus on God, not on yourself. God's purposes will be accomplished -- and He will use you as you use your spiritual gifts!

Day 4 - What God Has Prepared for Us

Scripture: 1 Corinthians 12:18; Ephesians 1:3-4

Somehow, many of us have failed to recognize the glory that God has attached to the church. Too often we see it as a thing we "ought to belong to," for family or social reasons. We want our kids to grow up to be good people, and we think maybe the church can help. Or we want to make friends with respectable people, so we try to find a church that is friendly and yet doesn't require too much of us.

God has a different view of His church. It is the Bride of Christ, made up of people He called into it by deliberate choice. God has called us personally and individually.

But now God has placed the members, each one of them, in the body, just as He desired. (1 Corinthians 12:18)

The church is God's creation, to be used in this day to carry out His redemptive purpose in the world. And He has chosen you and me to be part of it. The choice was not accidental. He chose us before the foundation of the world to be holy and blameless, to be adopted as His children, to serve Him and to be a part of His great redemptive plan.

What does this truth do for your self-esteem? The way you see yourself should be settled once and for all! God sees you as a vital part of His plan. Is anything more important in all the world than being a part of God's plan? Write a sentence to describe how this makes you feel right now.

_____

_____

Pray that God will help you understand just how much He loves you and why He has called you to be a part of the body of Christ for this time.

Day 5 - The God of the Mouth

Scripture: Exodus 3:1 - 4:12

During the past few days, you've read much about Moses and his encounter with God in the burning bush. God has a remarkable way of getting someone's attention, doesn't He?

Moses struggled with God about going before Pharaoh, but in the struggle Moses learned that God never purposes anything He is not prepared to accomplish by His mighty power. God sent Moses, but it wasn't Moses who delivered the people. It was God. And in a climactic moment of this marvelous story, Moses protests that he is unable to speak effectively -- either to Pharaoh or to the people. God reminds him:

> *"Who has made man's mouth? Or who makes him dumb or deaf, or seeing or blind? Is it not I, the Lord? Now then go, and I, even I, will be with your mouth, and teach you what you are to say."* (Exodus 4:11-12)

If you have been afraid to speak for God, what has stood in your way? _____
How could God have overcome it?_____

Determine right now that you are going to learn from God what He has gifted you to do, and how He expects you to use your gifts for His glory. Responsibility for your success in speaking the truth belongs to God! Trust Him.

Pray now that you will learn the same lessons Moses learned. Like Moses, you can become a servant of God.

Lesson 2

THE GIVER OF GIFTS

Now there are varieties of gifts, but the same Spirit.   1 Corinthians 12:4

KEY THOUGHT

God created you in His image and gave you spiritual gifts to serve alongside Him for the redemption of the world.

OUTLINE OF VIDEO LESSON

1. Too many Christians want to know their spiritual _____ instead of wanting to know the _____.

2. Paul uses two different Greek words that are translated "spiritual gifts." The first is *pneumatakoi* (1 Cor. 12:1), which means "manifestation of the spirit." The Corinthians applied this term to the obvious, outwardly visible gifts. Paul answers the Corinthians' question by substituting the term *charismata* (1 Cor. 12:4), which means "manifestations of grace." The Corinthians wanted to be known as spiritual people (another translation of *pneumatakoi*); Paul wanted them to refocus on the source -- the Giver -- rather than on the impression they made on one another. Gifts prove nothing about the possessor, but everything about the Giver. God graciously _____ His people.

3. Key scriptures describing spiritual gifts have different ways of identifying the giver:

    In 1 Corinthians 12:4-ff, the giver is the _____ _____.

    In Romans 12:3, the giver is _____.

    In Ephesians 4:7, the giver is _____.

4. The entire _____ was involved in gifting you for effective service. God has gifted you to participate with Him in the work He began in His Son and that He wants to complete in His _____.

5. Seven components of healthy, _____ self-esteem are: 1) <u>inherent worth</u>, 2) a <u>sense of security</u>, 3) a <u>strong self-concept</u>, 4) a <u>sense of purpose</u>, 5) a <u>sense of belonging</u>, 6) a <u>sense of empowerment</u>, and 7) <u>personal competence</u>.

CONFESSION

I, _____,

am created in the image of God, redeemed by the grace of God,

filled and gifted by the Spirit of God, and chosen by the hand of

God to serve alongside Him for the redemption of the world.

---

1. ***Sarah Monroe*** *grew up in a military family, graduated with honors from The American University in Paris, and subsequently landed a job in international banking in Florida. Her family had moved eleven times during her school years, but she had handled the moves well and was a confident, outgoing person who never met a stranger.*

   She began attending a Bible study luncheon with two business colleagues and eventually made a commitment to Christ. Sarah's life began changing immediately. She discovered a new way of thinking, made new friends and began studying the Bible. Suddenly the whole idea of church began to make sense to her as a place to grow spiritually. Her heart became sensitive to needs that were mentioned.

   Soon Sarah realized that her two Christian friends were more than just attendees at church. They were active participants. In fact, they were leaders. They gave hours of their time to planning sessions, participated in decision making, led out in special projects, even received considerable recognition for their efforts. Sarah began hearing phrases like "working together"..."making a difference by using our gifts"..."ministry needs"..."spiritual gifts" ..."fulfillment." She began asking herself some serious questions.

   What do you think was going through her mind? Write down 4 or 5 questions she might have begun asking herself.

   _____

   _____

   _____

   _____

2. What do you think are some factors that motivated Sarah to take this deeper look into herself?

   _____

   _____

3. Read Romans 12:1-2 and discuss what these phrases mean to you. Make some notes.

   "present your bodies" -_____

   "spiritual service of worship" - _____

   "be not conformed to the world" -_____

   "be transformed" - _____

   "renewing of your mind" - _____

   "proving what the will of God is" - _____

   "good, acceptable and perfect" - _____

4. If God commands us "to _____ our bodies...be transformed by the _____ of our minds...so we can _____ what is the good and acceptable and perfect _____ of God," it stands to reason that He equips us for the "spiritual _____" Paul states in verse 1. What does the term "spiritual service" suggest to you?

   _____

5. In 1 Corinthians 12:7 and following, Paul gives us insight into how God equips us for service. He says that "to each one is given the manifestation (outward evidence) of the Spirit

for the _____ _____" and then talks about our being "members of _____ body."

What do you feel is the overall truth of this passage, and how does it relate to you and your church?

_____

_____

6. How should we as Christians feel about ourselves knowing that we are the recipients of God's gifts and important members of the body of Christ?

_____

_____

7. When we learn that there are needs within the body that must be addressed or members who need help, we should:

_____

_____.

8. As Sarah Monroe grew spiritually, she began to think with a _____ mind, see through different _____ and hear through different _____. She was touched by the needs she saw around her and began to realize that perhaps she could begin channeling her efforts to meet some of those needs. The _____ of gifts had endowed her just as He had endowed her friends.

9. When I, _____ (your name) gratefully acknowledge that the _____ of gifts has endowed me with gifts to be used for service within the _____ of Christ, it gives me a feeling of true significance. I am literally in partnership with God. As I respond to Him with a renewed mind and begin to function within the area of my giftedness, I open wide the windows of my potential to _____ _____!

10. Now turn back to the video outline and read the confession together out loud.

PERSONAL APPLICATION

1. Write one thought or insight that God has impressed upon your heart during this lesson.

2. Identify at least one commitment you expect to make as a result of this lesson.

MICKAY MINNIE serves God out of a heart filled with gratitude. God has given her an outstanding Christian husband, two fine sons and many friends. He has also given her a church where she can channel her energies for the highest of all purposes. She feels that serving God is simply the natural expression of her life ever since the day she received Christ.

Like many Christians, Mickay is sensitive to the needs of people, but she puts her sensitivity into action. She will step forward at the drop of a hat to help meet the needs of others, even when it is inconvenient for her to do so. She takes food to families with illness, keeps children while other parents tend to emergencies, runs errands for friends who need assistance, helps with baby showers for young mothers who might otherwise be overlooked, not to mention caring for her own family and handling responsibilities at church.

Whether it's teaching in Sunday School or helping with churchwide projects, she takes every invitation to serve seriously. Her attitude is, "I'd better consider this. It may be a wonderful opportunity to serve the Lord."

Mickay has learned that even though meaningful service often involves personal sacrifice, the satisfaction received is worth far more than the effort expended. She feels that Christians should be willing to go the second mile for others and for the Lord.

The spirit of unselfish, unrecognized service is just the opposite of what Paul faced as he wrote his first letter to the Corinthians. He was responding to some mistaken ideas about what it means to be a spiritual person. In 1 Corinthians 12:1, he answers something the Corinthians had asked about. The Greek word translated "spiritual gifts" could also mean "spiritual persons," and some members of the church at Corinth considered themselves a cut above their brethren because they saw themselves as more spiritual.

Do you see anything like this in your church? Have you ever known people who just feel they have an extra special touch of the Holy Spirit, and want everyone else to think so? Have you ever been tempted to feel this way? God has given spiritual gifts to *all* His children, and He has a great eternal purpose for giving those gifts.

The failure to realize that we are all gifted by God is a significant factor in the lack of power in the church today. Along with spiritual gifts themselves, God also gives the power to use the gifts. But it is not really our power that is at work. It is God's supernatural power that enables us to use the gifts He gives. His power overcomes all of our weaknesses.

God has a plan and a purpose for you, and He provides the power you need. As you pursue the truth of God's Word concerning spiritual gifts, try to focus on the *Giver* -- not on the gifts. The gifts (*charismata*) are the results of His grace (*charis*). The gifts prove how gracious God is, not how great we are. The gifts are His way of equipping you, empowering you, and encouraging you! You're important to Him. Don't miss what He has uniquely prepared for you.

DAILY BIBLE STUDIES

Day 1 - When Did God Choose You?
Scripture: Jeremiah 1:5

God starts His planning very early. Jeremiah 1:5 shows how God's sovereign purposes are ordered and set in place:

"Before I formed you in your mother's womb I knew you,
And before you were born I consecrated you..."

Jeremiah didn't choose God. God chose Jeremiah, just as He chose you. God deals with us the same way. Before you were formed in your mother's womb, God knew how you fit into His plan. He needs you to make the plan complete. You are essential!

Jeremiah was a man whose heart could be broken over the sins of God's people. God's message called for a broken heart -- a heart that could weep and pray without ceasing, in holy intercession for a people chosen by God to serve Him. Can you see how your character, your personality, your heart can be shaped by God for a purpose in His kingdom?

What would it take right now for God to prepare you for service?_____

God gave you gifts to enable you to carry out His assignment. These gifts are the keys to fulfilling all He has in store for you.

Ask God to reveal to you how He has gifted you, and be prepared to respond obediently.

Day 2 - The Promise and the Power
Scripture: John 14:12

Jesus told His disciples that something incredible would happen to them. They had seen Him perform miracles -- healing, raising the dead, multiplying the fish and bread. Now He told them:

Truly, truly I say to you, he who believes in me, the works that I do shall he do also; and greater works than these shall he do; because I go to the Father. (John 14:12)

How do you think the disciples felt when they heard that? _____

Did Jesus really mean what He said? Could the disciples actually do more than He had done? He is God in the flesh! How could they possibly do more?

The answer lies in the last phrase of the statement: "Because I go to the Father." The purpose of His return to the Father was the sending of the Holy Spirit -- as teacher, helper, and power source. Because Jesus returned to the Father, you have the mighty power of the eternal God within you!

Is it true? Trust God and see. Open your mind and heart to what the Spirit wants to reveal to you.

Pray that God will show you what this can mean in your life.

Day 3 - Learning to Do All Things

Scripture: Philippians 4:13

Paul would have been extremely presumptuous if he had stopped in mid-sentence when he wrote Philippians 4:13 -- "I can do all things..." But God had worked powerfully in Paul's life, so Paul knew where his strength came from. He finished the statement: "...through Him who strengthens me."

This is the testimony of the life of every Christian who has experienced the strengthening power of God. Paul had been confronted by the Lord on the road to Damascus, had seen his life totally changed, and had learned the truth of the Christ's words: "Without me you can do nothing." (John 15:5)

The flip-side of this statement, however, is this: "*With* me you can do *anything*." This is what Paul was saying in Philippians 4:13. The strength that comes from God is real and available. He gives His strength for the accomplishing of His purposes. Anything God can do, He can do through you, because you have His strength available to you.

Has there been a time in your Christian life when you felt you could do **anything** because you had God's strength within you? Recall the occasion and write a brief description of it.

_____

_____

Be aware of what God is doing in your life! Acknowledge that He has prepared you, gifted you, and strengthened you. Discern His will, and be prepared to carry it out.

Pray that God will show you His will for your life and empower you with His strength to accomplish it. He is eager to do so.

Day 4 - What Does God Want to Do?

Scripture: Ephesians 3:1-12

Do you like a good mystery? God put one together that is a real mind-bender.

In Ephesians 3, Paul describes "the mystery which for ages has been hidden in God...." He explains the mystery: God intended from eternity to include the Gentiles -- the whole world -- as objects of His love in His plan of redemption. This truth sets firmly in place the mission of the church of Jesus Christ.

What do you think the church could or should do right now to help its members become aware of what God has planned for them? _____

_____

Who is the church? The church is you and me. It is everyone God has called and set apart for His use, as you saw in yesterday's Bible study. The purpose: *"that the manifold wisdom of God might now be made known **through the church** to the rulers and the authorities in the heavenly places."* (Ephesians 3:10). Your part is to accept what God has done, to yield to Him in faith and to give Him your life in service. He links you with the body, then equips you with spiritual gifts which are uniquely yours, and by which you can do all that He has purposed for you to do. Learn from Him, and let Him do His work through you!

Ask God to reveal how He has gifted you and what He wants to do in your life.

Day 5 - Fellow Heirs, Fellow Members, Fellow Partakers
Scripture: Ephesians 3:6

Look again at Paul's explanation of the *"mystery of Christ, which in former generations was not made known to the sons of men...."* (Ephesians 3:4,5) It was indeed a mystery, but not simply a set of hidden facts which God had withheld from His people.

The mystery of Christ is that God had purposed from before He created the world that He would enter the life of mankind as God in the flesh -- in the person of Jesus Christ -- as the full and final work of redemption for a lost world. God had chosen the people of Israel to be the family into which His Son would be born. He had given them His truth through many generations so that they could be prepared to respond at the appearing of the Lord of Glory. But His intent all along was that "all nations would be blessed" by Israel, that the Gentiles would become God's people as fully as had Israel. He would be the God of **all** of His creation.

Paul makes it clear that in Christ...

"...the Gentiles are fellow heirs and fellow members of the body, and fellow partakers of the promise in Christ Jesus through the gospel...." (Ephesians 3:6)

In the unveiling of this mystery, the church was born and received its mission. It is God's purpose that all people hear and respond to the call of Jesus Christ to repentance and salvation.

This is not to be a matter of pride for the non-Jew. It is rather an affirmation of the original, gracious, all-inclusive plan of God -- that His creation would be redeemed and restored to its original purpose and that all who come to Him in faith would enjoy His presence and blessing forever.

This is the purpose of His gifts, His mercy, His provision. It is His purpose in your life. What obligation do you think this places on you?_____
_____

Ask God to continue to shape your life with His wisdom and truth as you seek to discover and use your spiritual gifts in His service.

Lesson 3

GOD'S PLAN AND PURPOSE FOR YOU

...I was made a minister, according to the gift of God's grace which was given to me according to the working of His power. To me, the very least of all saints, this grace was given, to preach to the Gentiles the unfathomable riches of Christ, and to bring to light what is the administration of the mystery which for ages has been hidden in God, who created all things; in order that the manifold wisdom of God might now be made known through the church to the rulers and the authorities in the heavenly places. This was in accordance with the eternal purpose which He carried out in Christ Jesus our Lord... Ephesians 3:7-11

KEY THOUGHT

God's plan and purpose is to work through you to reveal Himself to the world around you.

OUTLINE OF VIDEO LESSON

1. God created you in His image so that you could have a relationship with _____, and as a result have a relationship with your _____ _____.

2. We were created to serve alongside Him, participating in His creative and _____ activity.

3. What God began in Christ He continues in the _____.

4. As Paul describes the gifted church in Ephesians 4:1-16, he shows that the exalted Christ gives the _____. The pastor/teacher equips the saints.

5. Five reasons why you should want to know your spiritual gifts:

    1) They are expressions of the Father's love.

    2) They enable you to fulfill the purpose for which God created you.

    3) They give meaning to your life and to your participation in the body of Christ.

    4) They enrich your personal life.

    5) They enhance the unity and effectiveness of your church.

1. Do you remember when you first began hearing a pastor or teacher tell you that God had a wonderful plan and purpose for you life? Do you remember how old you were and how it made you feel? Share together and make some notes.

    _____

    _____

    As you have gotten older, has the truth that God does have a plan and purpose for your life become more real to you? How have you been able to see God's hand in your life, working things together for good according to His purpose? (Romans 8:28)

    _____

    _____

2. *Bob Raymond is 57 years old and feels that he has just begun discovering God's plan and purpose for his life.*

    He grew up in a devout, but rigid, Christian home with a domineering mother and an absentee father who soon deserted them. When he left home as a young man, Bob headed in the wrong direction and wound up managing night clubs in upstate New York. He was very well-paid and considered highly successful at what he did. He married young, had two children, became an alcoholic and eventually divorced.

    At age 39, Bob got some help with his drinking problem and never wavered from that time on. Eventually he started going to church. The one thing that still seemed to evade him, however, was the thought planted in the back of his mind years ago that God had a plan and purpose for his life. Life was slipping by and he still hadn't found his niche of satisfaction. Things just were not panning out. Something was missing.

    At age 55, things began to change for Bob, and he began the journey toward the fulfilling life he has today.

    What do you think happened? Use your imagination and bring Bob's story up to date.

3. Do you believe most Christians have a clear grasp of God's plan and purpose for their lives? Why or why not?

    _____

4. Think for a moment of some specific individuals you know who seem to be fulfilling God's purpose with their lives. Write their names down, along with a note or two describing why you feel this way about them. Discuss.

    _____

    _____

    _____

5. Read Ephesians 4:1-16 together and select words or phrases that relate to God's plan and purpose for our lives. What does the passage say about:

    *   Our calling? _____

    *   Our attitudes? _____

    *   Our actions? _____

    *   The source of gifts? _____

- The purpose of gifts? _____
- What we are to strive for and attain? _____
- The church? _____

6. Based on the above passage:

It is clear to me that God does have an overall _____ for my life. I am to walk in a manner _____ of my calling. He did not design me to function as an island unto myself, but as an integral member of a body of believers who are _____ by God to serve together in the building up of the church. God's plan for me is to grow and mature in my faith in Him, not to be knocked around by wrong influences and false belief systems. All the while I will recognize _____ as the head. The end result of my carrying out God's purpose for my life is the growth of the church so it can be built up in _____.

7. Really, there can be no greater _____!

PERSONAL APPLICATION

1. Write one thought or insight that God has impressed upon your heart during this lesson.

2. Identify at least one commitment you expect to make as a result of this lesson.

JAMES AND CAROL BLAND, a neurosurgeon and his wife, had been out of church for about 15 years. A successful medical practice and family responsibilities kept them busy during the week, and recreation kept them busy on weekends.

One day they visited church services at the invitation of an anesthesiologist friend, and they enjoyed a refreshing experience they'd not had in many years. They continued visiting, made new friends, and eventually joined.

As they became active and began to grow spiritually, they let it be known that they were willing to reach out to others the same way the church had reached out to them. They had no real preferences as to where they wanted to serve; they just wanted to make a difference with their lives.

Because they were flexible and had a willing spirit, they were recruited to serve in several areas. They served on strategic committees, led an adult Sunday School class, served in Vacation Bible School, led fund-raising campaigns, represented the church at special mission functions, and eventually James became a deacon.

All the Blands wanted to do was to give back to God some of what He had given to them. Their new sense of belonging and renewal motivated them to serve joyfully wherever there was a need. Their lives continue making a difference today.

This is just one illustration of the church fulfilling God's purposes - one Christian reaching out to another, drawing him into a fellowship, an inviting atmosphere where spiritual renewal can take place.

How can we define the church, and why is it important in God's plan? The church is God's instrument for carrying out His redemptive purpose in our age. Every member of the church has been placed there by God's sovereign choice (1 Cor. 12:18) for the purpose of working alongside Him in the redemption of the world. This includes you.

Paul's letter to the Ephesians gives us a startling picture. He says that for centuries God had hidden one part of His plan, waiting to reveal it through the person and ministry of His Son, Jesus Christ. Jesus would provide the full manifestation of who God is and what He has planned for His people. By His life and teaching, He would reveal God's original purpose: that believers in the one God from all peoples and nations would share in His gifts and blessings:

> *...in order that the manifold wisdom of God might now be made known through the church to the rulers and the authorities in the heavenly places.* (Ephesians 3:10)

The church is the body of Christ, active in the world while He is at the right hand of the Father. Just as God gave you a body, He gave his Son this body, the church.

In the next lesson, you will have a closer look at the spiritual gifts which, when exercised by the members, make the body function as God intends. You will gain a better understanding of the gifts and how they can be used in joyful service to God and the church. Like every other child of God, you have been gifted by God for this purpose.

Day 1 - God's Great Guarantee
Scripture: Matthew 16:18

We live in a day when people have learned not to trust each other too much. As unfortunate as this may seem, it is probably a reasonable response to an age of deception.

Can you trust anybody? Can you hang your hat on anything anybody says?

The Word of God has proven trustworthy for centuries. Jesus said (Matthew 24:35): *"Heaven and earth will pass away, but My words shall not pass away."* His words are powerful and eternal. Simon Peter declared that Jesus is *"the Christ, the Son of the living God."* Jesus replied:

"Blessed are you, Simon Barjona, because flesh and blood did not reveal this to you, but My Father who is in heaven. And I say to you that you are Peter, and upon this rock I will build My church; and the gates of Hades shall not overpower it."
(Matthew 16:17-18)

Jesus said "the church is mine; I will build it, and the enemy cannot stand against it." The church is us -- you and me -- and it will accomplish God's purposes.

Do you feel that the members of your church recognize themselves as the body of Christ, with individual parts working together according to God's purpose? Write your thoughts about this. _____

_____

Ask God to enable you to hear His voice as He shows you what He has planned for you. Pray for the will to respond in faith and walk in His power.

Day 2 - The Pillar and Support of the Truth
Scripture: 1 Timothy 3:14-15

The Gospels describe the life of the Christ and His work in establishing His church. The letters of Paul teach us how to function as members of the church:

I write so that you may know how one ought to conduct himself in the household of God, which is the church of the living God, the pillar and support of the truth."
(1 Tim. 3:14-15)

Paul had just given Timothy specific instructions concerning prayer, evangelism and discipleship. His words are for us as well. We are to pray for all men, because all men are precious to God, ...*who desires all men to be saved and to come to the knowledge of the truth.* (1 Tim. 2:4) God's desire is for all men to know Him through an experience of salvation in Jesus Christ. This is the mission of the church. Thus it is **your** work.

Write here the name of a friend who may not know Jesus Christ as Savior. Make a commitment to speak to that friend this week about Christ. Also write his or her response here before the next session.

_____ _____

_____

Pray that God will give you wisdom and courage as you prepare for this important task.

Day 3 - A Member of the Body
Scripture: 1 Corinthians 12:27

Paul writes to the church at Corinth:

Now you are Christ's body, and individually members of it. (1 Corinthians 12:27)

Was there ever a clearer statement of what it means to belong to the church of the living God? We are the very body of the Lord Jesus Christ. You may be a hand, or an eye, or a knee. The fact is inescapable. You are someone special in the body of Christ!

Can you know what your function is? Can an individual really discover what specific role he or she should play in the working of the church of today? And if so, how?

The answer lies in an awareness, a study, an acceptance of the fact that God has given spiritual gifts to each member of the body. He does this *"for the common good"* (1 Cor. 12:7). The common good requires that each member function in a specific way, so that the whole body works as a single organism. Only then can the body carry out God's purposes in the world.

If the foot should say, "Because I am not a hand, I am not a part of the body," it is not for this reason any less a part of the body. (1 Cor. 12:15)

Does it seem to you that some gifts are more important to the body than others? Why?

_____

_____

Have you ever felt that your role in the church is less important than others?

We cannot escape responsibility by feeling that we are not as important as another member of the body. God says the foot is as important as the hand. Whatever your gift equips you to do is God's assignment for you in the church.

Pray that God will show you how important it is for you to know your part in the body. Pray for the will to function in that capacity to the best of your ability.

Day 4 - Gifts That Differ
Scripture: Romans 12:4-6

Have you begun to look around your church to guess who has which gifts? Are other people looking at you, wondering the same thing? Are you looking at yourself?

Spiritual gifts are not always easy to identify. The Bible contains more than one list of gifts, and the lists do not agree at all points. In addition, some people have concluded that there is a significant difference between spiritual gifts and natural talents. Is it possible that your natural talents are indeed gifts of God, given by Him so that you can serve Him? You'll learn more about this in the next lesson.

God wants you to accept and respect the differences among members of the church. No gift is more important in the sight of God than another. He uses each person in a unique way to make the body function at full power and to maximum effect.

Many people in your church are very different from you. The Holy Spirit has given them gifts that are different from yours -- not more or less important, but different. Write the names of some of these individuals in the space provided, then pray for them by name.

You have gifts that are unique to you. Pray that God will show you what your gift is and how you are to use it to bring honor and glory to Him.

Day 5 - Living With the Gifts
Scripture: Romans 12:4-21

In the human arena, we are prone to focus on the gift we receive rather than on the giver. In the realm of spiritual gifts, this is a danger not to be taken lightly.

The focus of the believer's life must always be on the giver. God's gifts are evidences of His love and purpose for us. His gifts prepare us to serve in His all-embracing plan of redemption.

Paul in his letter to the Romans moves immediately from a discussion of the spiritual gifts (Romans 12:4-8) to a highly-charged presentation of proper Christian behavior (Romans 12:9-21). He allows no room for self-importance or for pride of possession where the spiritual gifts are concerned.

Paul insists on a pattern of life that calls for the best we can do with any kind of giftedness. He speaks of devotion to one another, honoring one another, being diligent, fervent, generous, hospitable. He calls for us to endure persecution in good spirit. He encourages unity of mind and purpose among believers.

He shows us how to live. He gives us a pattern for servanthood that is a model for all the world. This is a true picture of the kind of life the spiritual gifts should produce in us.

Has there been an occasion recently when you didn't give everything God called for in terms of energy, time, or talent? Write your thoughts about this experience.

_____
_____
_____

Pray that God will show you a better way.

Lesson 4

UNDERSTANDING SPIRITUAL GIFTS

But to each one is given the manifestation of the Spirit for the common good.
1 Corinthians 12:7

And since we have gifts that differ according to the grace given to us, let each exercise them accordingly. Romans 12:6

KEY THOUGHT

A spiritual gift (charismata) is an individualized manifestation of grace from the Father that enables you to serve Him and thus play a vital role in His plan for the redemption of the world.

OUTLINE OF VIDEO LESSON

1. Three reasons why so few Christians recognize their spiritual giftedness are:

    1) failure to _____

    2) fear of the unknown

    3) the fog factor, which includes confusion about the _____ and nature of gifts in the Bible; linking spiritual gifts with personality temperaments; and uncertainty about the relationship of spiritual gifts with natural talents

2. Paul's lists of gifts in 1 Corinthians, Romans, and Ephesians should not be understood as comprehensive, but rather as _____ or illustrative.

3. God always gifts His church to do what He has _____ it to do in any generation.

4. The number of gifts is dependent upon the need of the church and the sovereign work of the _____ _____.

5. God will give a church the gift _____ needed to accomplish its purpose.

1. Let's review our definition of "spiritual gift." A spiritual gift is an _____
    manifestation (outward evidence) of _____ (unmerited, special favor) from the
    _____ that enables you to _____ Him and thus play a vital role in His plan
    for the _____ of the world.

2. Take a few moments to examine Paul's lists of gifts in 1 Corinthians 12:7-11, 1 Corinthians
    12:28, Romans 12:6-8 and Ephesians 4:11-12. What are your observations concerning:

    1) the churches Paul is writing?
    2) the lists themselves?
    3) purposes of the gifts?

    Why do you think Paul didn't give <u>one</u> comprehensive list and refer to the same list as he
    wrote different churches instead of varying the lists as he did?

    _____

    _____

3. When you recognize the vast differences between the world of Paul's day and the world we
    are living in, is it possible that some spiritual gifts might be needed today that were not
    needed in Paul's day?_____

    List some specific needs we have today that were probably not recognized needs in Paul's
    day?

    _____

    _____

    If God were to create new spiritual gifts to meet some of today's needs, what might they be?

    _____

    _____

4. Consider the following individuals and discuss some specific ways they can use their
    giftedness to serve God through the local church.

    > *Steve is an advanced computer consultant who is proficient installing, programming, and
    > operating mainframes or PCs. He is also a skilled TV cameraman and has a knack for
    > production and direction. He is willing to donate 4 to 6 hours per week to the church.*

    > *Suzanne is the leading sales agent for a large commercial real estate firm. One reason
    > she is so successful is that she is highly organized and offers a variety of attractive
    > financing options to her clients. Her church is considering either a total relocation or
    > starting a satellite church. She's a fairly new Christian.*

    > *George is a dentist who is semi-retired and looking for something meaningful to do with
    > his time. His pastor has made a appeal for volunteers to assist with mission projects in
    > South America, but participants must pay their own way.*

> ***Charles and Sue*** *have sold their landscape architecture firm and relocated to a small resort community where a new church is being organized. They've been active Christians for years. They serve as trustees of a children's home in their hometown.*

> ***Marta*** *has just taken a new position on the drama faculty with a local university. Her husband, Baxter, has assumed a position in advertising and design at an art institute in the same city. Baxter has been a deacon for six years.*

> ***Harold*** *is a consultant who helps companies develop leadership training programs for their employees. He also presents seminars on a variety of management topics and does some laypreaching.*

5. Divide your group into members of two imaginary churches. One church is located in an older declining part of town and has a membership made up primarily of senior adults. The other church is located in a dynamic area that is exploding with residential and commercial growth.

   Discuss how ministry needs and gift needs might differ between these two churches.

6. Read together again out loud our definition of a spiritual gift.

*A **spiritual gift** is an*
individualized manifestation of grace from the Father
that enables you to serve Him and thus play a vital role
in His plan for the redemption of the world.

PERSONAL APPLICATION

1. Write one thought or insight that God has impressed upon your heart during this lesson.

2. Identify at least one commitment you expect to make as a result of this lesson.

DAN TURNER, a self-taught mechanic who started out working on old cars, developed into a mechanical wizard. Tenneco, Inc. would fly him all over the United States whenever their big engines were not operating properly. It is said that he often diagnosed malfunctions of huge turbine engines costing hundreds of thousands of dollars by just standing close to them and listening for what other people could not hear.

When the church Dan belonged to announced it was starting a bus ministry to reach children no one else was reaching, he stepped forward. He casually mentioned he was a mechanic of sorts, and would like to help take care of the used school buses the church had purchased. Soon after Dan was welcomed into the bus ministry with open arms, he had the fleet of nine buses running smoothly. He devoted his Saturdays to bus repair.

It wasn't long before everyone realized that Dan had strong administrative skills as well as mechanical skills. Because he was highly organized and efficient, he was asked to serve as lay director of the ministry, and he accepted immediately. He shared that he had a growing burden for reaching children, received great satisfaction and fulfillment from it and had been praying that he would be given the opportunity to lead the ministry. In less than five months, he had the bus ministry bringing 350 children each week. Many of them subsequently received Christ and were baptized.

Dan Turner saw a need that soon became a burden. He then recognized his abilities and gifts and responded to the challenge to serve God. One year later he resigned his position with Tenneco and entered full-time Christian ministry.

―――――――――――――

Like Dan Turner, many a willing person has accepted a responsibility within the church without realizing just where it would lead. The Holy Spirit often takes an interest, a talent or an aptitude and leads an individual to a place of service where spiritual giftedness becomes evident.

Before we can discover how God has gifted us, we must understand what the gifts are. While the gifts listed in the New Testament met the needs of the church of Paul's day, do these lists contain all the gifts God may need for today's church? Doesn't it seem reasonable that He might supply additional spiritual gifts that are appropriate and necessary for today's needs?

Have we all been given spiritual gifts along with the new birth? Yes, we are all included in Paul's statement, *"But to each one is given the manifestation of the Spirit for the common good."* (1 Corinthians 12:7) *Each* means *every*. God has gifted every child of His for the common good. We are gifted for effective work in God's redemptive plan.

Knowing that we have a God who can do whatever He pleases, we should recognize how He has demonstrated His ways throughout history in dealing with His people. His way is to provide what is needed for the church to accomplish His will.

In the weeks ahead, you will discover how to identify and use your individual gifts to bring glory to the one who made you and gifted you.

Next week's lesson contains vital links between what you've already learned and what is to come. Before next week's lesson, spend time in the daily Bible studies that follow.

DAILY BIBLE STUDIES

Day 1 - God Makes the Choice
Scripture: 1 Corinthians 12:11, 18

Within a few short weeks, you will have discovered how God has gifted you for His service. You will be excited to realize that the eternal God has chosen you to join Him in His plan of world redemption. This is awesome!

Before you understand fully, you may look at your spiritual gift and ask, "Why did God give me this gift?"

The answer to your question: "You are sovereignly designed by God. This gift is designed for you individually. He has made no mistakes in placing that gift in you, then placing you in this body of Christ for His purposes. He puts the body together to match the assignment He has for it. And He puts the gift in you for the same reason. He expects you to respond by faithfully putting the gift to work in whatever direction He may lead you." You may need to make some significant changes in your life in order for the gift to be expressed in meaningful action.

You may become aware of something that is missing in your church. It may be a key slot in which an obedient, capable, and energetic individual could help the church to function more smoothly and efficiently. If that is the case, make a note of it here, and return to this page at the end of this study. Perhaps God is showing you something about your gift. What might it be?_____

_____

Ask God to help you discern the gift He has placed within you and understand why He has given it.

Day 2 - Using the Gifts: A Matter of Responsibility
Scripture: Romans 12:6-8

In the matter of spiritual gifts, Romans 12:6 is an especially important statement. It says:

And since we have gifts that differ according to the grace given to us, let each exercise them accordingly...

What does this scripture suggest to you? _____

_____

Our gifts *"differ according to the grace given to us."* God has specific gifts for each of us. These are *individual* gifts, matching what God has in mind as our function in the church. This is so that His redemptive purpose can be accomplished.

"Let us exercise them accordingly..." Let us act appropriately. Let us respond obediently in the light of God's grace in giving these gifts. He has honored us with His confidence. We owe Him our obedience.

Pray that God will demonstrate His grace in specific ways as He reveals your gift.

Day 3 - Comparing the Gifts

Scriptures: Romans 12:6-8; 1 Corinthians 12:8-10, 28; Ephesians 4:11

These passages are the principal biblical sources relating to activities referred to as spiritual gifts. They are specific, but different. Do you think they place a limit on the gifts that God is able to grant to His people? Are they comprehensive or representative?

As you seek an understanding of the spiritual gifts, you will want to study the lists carefully. Learn what they are and pray to understand why they were given. Note the duplications as well as the differences. Ask the Holy Spirit to help you grasp Paul's purpose and method in dealing with the different needs of the churches in Rome, Corinth and Ephesus. Keep these lists in mind as you continue this study and as you consider what other possibilities God may have in mind for preparing his people for service.

How many gifts do you see on all of the lists?_____ How many are included on more than one list?_____ Do you think the differences indicate that different churches need different gifts to carry out their assignments?_____.

Ask God to give you His special insight as you continue your study of the spiritual gifts and as you seek to determine your own giftedness.

Day 4 - The Goal of the Gifts

Scripture: Ephesians 4:13-16

Paul's intentions are very clear. He is giving instruction to all churches regarding the goal of the gifted ministry. The goal is doctrinal integrity. This was a concern for Paul in the first century A.D. and is a concern for the church today. The churches then were guided primarily by the early writings of Paul and the other Apostles. Many of them also had the teachings of those who had been with Jesus. But there were two threats to the doctrinal strength of the churches back then. There were false teachers whose aims were self-serving. And there were divisions within the churches caused by power-seeking church leaders.

Doctrinal integrity was and is vital. Paul wanted to be sure that his explanation of the gifts would make the church fully aware of its responsibility in using the gifts. The gifted ministry of the New Testament church must pay attention to its own maturity in the faith. The key to this passage is 4:13:

...until we all attain to the unity of the faith, and of the knowledge of the Son of God, to a mature man, to the measure of the stature which belongs to the fullness of Christ.

How do you think the gifts would enable the church to achieve unity in the faith?_____
_____
_____

The exercise of the gifts in the body would make possible a growing knowledge of Christ Himself, with a result that the church would become mature. It would grow up and achieve a stature worthy of the Lord Jesus. His desire was and is that His body would be mature as He is mature.

That is the goal toward which every church today must direct its growth plan. Not more numbers, but true spiritual maturity. That is the primary step in our use of the spiritual gifts.

Pray that you and your church will discover your gifts and use them to reach this maturity.

Day 5 -- Barnabas: The Encourager
Scripture: Acts 11:23-24

A good way to understand the giving and proper use of spiritual gifts is by studying the Bible characters who best display those gifts. Barnabas is one such personality. Barnabas had the gift of *exhortation*, or encouragement *(Romans 12:8)*.

You can learn about Barnabas in Acts 4:36, 37; 9:27 - 15:39. Also, he is mentioned in 1 Corinthians 9:6, Galatians 2:1,9,13; and Colossians 4:10.

The key passage for our purpose is found in Acts 11:23 and 24:

Then when he (Barnabas) had come and witnessed the grace of God, he rejoiced and began to encourage them all with resolute heart to remain true to the Lord; for he was a good man, and full of the Holy Spirit and of faith. And considerable numbers were brought to the Lord.

What a testimony to a man's life! Barnabas made effective use of his spiritual gift. It was through the exercise of this gift that others could see that he was "full of the Holy Spirit and of faith." Many people came to know the Lord Jesus because Barnabas allowed the Spirit of God to show him his gift, and then empower him to use the gift in service to God.

This is God's desired result for all of us: *to be involved in His redemptive plan through the exercise of our gifts, given to us individually by His grace.*

Are there some "Barnabas" type people in your church? People whose lives are an encouragement to everyone they meet?

Write some of their names here. _____
_____
_____

Make it a point to tell them how much it means to you to witness their encouraging spirit.

Pray that God will make you an encourager of everyone you meet, regardless of the specific nature of your spiritual gift. Pray that because of your witness, "considerable numbers will be brought to the Lord."

Lesson 5

UNDERSTANDING YOUR SPIRITUAL GIFTEDNESS

...since you are zealous of spiritual gifts, seek to abound for the edification of the church. 1 Corinthians 14:12

KEY THOUGHT

Your spiritual gift is an individualized endowment of grace that will enable you to serve God by building up others.

OUTLINE OF VIDEO LESSON

1. You need to ask yourself, "What is my _____ for seeking my gift?"

2. In Corinth, Paul indicated that many in the church were seeking to discover their spiritual gifts to prove that they were _____.

3. Beginning in 1 Corinthians 14:12, Paul shows that the Christian is to seek after spiritual gifts for the edification of the _____.

4. Your gift is _____, working through your personality, history, experience, and passion, all in the context of ministry to enable you to serve God effectively.

5. Six important principles of spiritual giftedness:

    1) The surrendered _____ (Romans 12:1)
    2) The renewed _____ (Romans 12:2-3)
    3) Universal _____ (Romans 12:6)
    4) Unity in _____ (Romans 12:4)
    5) _____ (Romans 12:5)
    6) _____ (Romans 12:7-10)

6. Through your gift you can touch the _____ and impact _____.

1. A young minister of music was doing everything he could to recruit new choir members for his adult choir. A respected person in the church recommended that he talk to **Jack Harwell** immediately. Jack supposedly had a tremendous voice, a great personality and was ready to get involved in the church. The minister of music talked to Jack after a morning service and applied some pressure for him to join the choir. Jack's wife overheard the conversation and quickly stepped in, insisting it would be a huge mistake for her husband to join the choir, even though he did love to sing. She said the problem was...he could not carry a tune! The wife's opinion was overridden by some friends standing by, and the minister of music proudly signed up a new baritone. With a heart full of enthusiasm, a broad smile on his face and an extremely loud voice, Jack joyfully made his musical contribution in choir the next Sunday morning.

    The only problem was, Jack _____!
    And he sang _____!

2. List some reasons why people might agree to serve in areas for which they are not really suited or gifted. What does this say about their positive attitude of willingness?

    _____

    _____

    _____

    Is it possible that their spirit of willingness is an indication that they are searching for a place to serve and might be open to training? Discuss. Share some examples.

3. Why it is important for individuals to serve in areas where they feel capable and confident? Discuss some factors that build confidence in volunteer leaders. Make notes.

    _____

    _____

    _____

4. The following positions or ministries are commonly found in many churches. What are some personality characteristics and areas of giftedness you feel would be appropriate for individuals to serve effectively in these positions and ministries? Choose five or six to discuss. Be specific.

    - Sunday School teacher - _____
    - Sunday School director - _____
    - Choir member - _____
    - Decision counselor - _____
    - Women's Bible study instructor - _____
    - Deacon - _____
    - Nursery worker - _____
    - Bus ministry - _____
    - Evangelism/outreach - _____
    - Youth sponsor - _____
    - Benevolence ministry - _____
    - Audio/visual/PA system - _____
    - Homebound ministry - _____
    - Overseas mission projects - _____
    - Prison ministry - _____
    - Ushers/Greeters - _____

5. We learned in our first lesson that two of the main reasons why people don't serve the Lord are 1) they don't feel _____, and 2) they don't feel _____.

    Is it possible that there are some other reasons why people don't serve the Lord through the local church? If so, list and discuss some of them.

    _____

    _____

6. Discuss some things we as Christians and as church leaders can do to encourage people to become involved in a place of service.

    _____

    _____

7. "Why" we do what we do is sometimes more important than "what" we do. Why is our motive for seeking to understand our spiritual gifts so important to a life of fulfilling service to God?

    _____

    _____

8. Jack Harwell dropped out of choir after three weeks (probably due to the prayers of the minister of music and the two guys on either side of him), but he didn't drop out of church. To the contrary, he was promptly asked to be a director of a new adult Sunday School department, a position which he accepted and excelled at!

    Why do you think this story had a happy ending instead of an unhappy one? Who do you think were the key players and what were their roles?

    _____

    _____

9. In summary, 1 Corinthians 14:12 tells us that our zeal to know our spiritual gifts must be motivated by our desire to contribute to the _____ of the church. This is the main reason why we should want to gain an understanding of our spiritual giftedness.

PERSONAL APPLICATION

1. Write one thought or insight that God has impressed upon your heart during this lesson.

2. Identify at least one commitment you expect to make as a result of this lesson.

JOE HIGHT, retired president of Dun & Bradstreet, joined a fast-growing new church where he thought he could make a difference with his life. With a proven track record in business and financial services, he wanted to channel his broad experience to help this congregation get off the ground and capture the opportunity of reaching multitudes of people for Christ.

Usually dressed informally, Joe was in and out of the church most every day helping direct financial matters at a time when money was spread thinly over staff, buildings, and new ministries.

But when it came time to go to the big downtown banks to try to persuade them to lend serious money to a fledgling congregation, he always dressed in banker's blue. He wanted his presence to match a polished presentation, thereby reflecting the seriousness of what he was about with his life and what his church was about in terms of ministry and growth.

What was Joe Hight's motivation? Recognition, praise, approval? No. He'd enjoyed plenty of that in the business world. His motivation now was to find fulfillment by serving the Lord with the special abilities and gifts he had developed over the years. His goal now was to help direct the church into a position of financial stability that would enable growth to continue for years to come.

That church will always owe a debt of gratitude to the "serve God" spirit of Joe Hight.

Whether it's in the area of church finance, music, or outreach, our motivation -- the "why" of what we do -- is a key factor in our effectiveness. Only when our motives are right can we be sure that our spiritual gifts can be fully surrendered and used by God. The key principles of spiritual giftedness that you learned in this lesson will help you in discovering your gift. The principles are found in Romans 12:1-8:

1. The principle of *the surrendered body* (Romans 12:2)
2. The principle of *the renewed mind* (Romans 12:2)
3. The principle of *universal giftedness* (Romans 12:6; 1 Corinthians 12:6,7)
4. The principle of *unity in diversity* (Romans 12:4,5)
5. The principle of *interdependence* (Romans 12:4,5; 1 Corinthians 12:14-27)
6. The principle of *service* (Romans 12:7-10; 1 Corinthians 14:12)

In concluding this week's study, repeat the prayer of commitment from the video:

A Prayer in Preparation for Discovery of Spiritual Gifts

Lord, I give you my body. I'm not seeking gifts for my own amusement, but for your service. I will rejoice in my gift, and use it to serve you. In Jesus' name. Amen.

Next week you will focus on some simple steps to help you discover your spiritual gift. These steps include: 1) discerning, 2) surrendering/empowering, and 3) developing your gift to use in service. You will also be given a "Personal Assessment Guide" to assist you in the discovery process. Remember your daily Bible studies this week, and pray for God's guidance as you prepare for the next lesson.

DAILY BIBLE STUDIES

Day 1 - What Has God Prepared for You?
Scripture: 1 Corinthians 2:9-16

We return to our starting point in this study of spiritual gifts. 1 Corinthians 2:9 says:

"Things which eye has not seen and ear has not heard, and which have not entered into the heart of man, all that God has prepared for those who love Him."

Paul is quoting the prophet Isaiah. The fact that Paul is repeating a truth that God had declared centuries earlier gives added emphasis. For Paul, there was something powerful in that promise. God has prepared things for those who love Him which are truly beyond human imagination.

Do you believe this? Paul puts it within the context of God's act in giving us His Holy Spirit as our link with Himself. He is our guide, comforter and power source. We receive from the Holy Spirit the gifts that are the subjects of our study together. And Paul is saying in the next verses (10-13) that the Spirit is given so that "we might *know the things freely given to us by God*." That includes our spiritual gifts.

How do you think God will reveal your gift to you? _____
_____

Are you prepared to accept the knowledge of your gift as a supernatural provision of God for your life of service to Him?_____. What should your response be?_____
_____.

Ask God to allow you a glimpse of His purpose in giving you the specific gifts that allow you to fulfill His purpose in your life.

Day 2 - God Wants You to Know and Understand
Scripture: 1 Corinthians 2:10-12

Let your mind be open to the mind of God as you consider this passage once more. His is a mind that is unsearchable by any human means. Yet Paul says that the Spirit of God who lives within us searches "even the depths of God" (vs. 10). What is the purpose of this searching?

As remarkable as it may seem, the Holy Spirit is searching the depths of God so "that we might know the things freely given to us by God." God is setting his own Spirit free to share with us what is on His heart and in His plan for us in union with Him. The Holy Spirit of God is our teacher and God's interpreter to us. He is preparing us for service.

How? By making certain that we discover and put to use our spiritual gifts. God wants us to know our gifts and then to take our place within the body of Christ in active exercise of those gifts for His glory. We need to know our spiritual gifts. He makes certain that we do.

Think of an individual you know whose spiritual gift you can identify, and whose life demonstrates the effective use of the gift. Write down the name of the person and the gift.
_____. What are the evidences that the gift is being well used in that person's life?

Pray for God's wisdom and understanding as you discover and begin to apply your gift in the life of your church.

Day 3 - The Things Freely Given
Scriptures: 1 Corinthians 2:12

When God gives, the deed is done and is not to be undone. This firmness of purpose and of action on God's part gives us all the assurance we need concerning our salvation, our justification, our sanctification, and our provision. What God has given us is ours and nothing can take it from us.

So it is with your spiritual gifts. You need to recognize how permanent your spiritual gifts are and how securely they belong to you. The key verse here is 1 Corinthians 2:12. It is a remarkable statement from the Apostle:

Now we have received, not the spirit of the world, but the Spirit who is from God, that we might know the things freely given to us by God.

Your giftedness is a manifestation of the Holy Spirit in you. It is yours. God plants it there "for the common good." He gives it for the good of the body of Christ. And your gifts are for the use of your surrendered body and renewed mind in service to God through the body.

Why do you think it is important to know that the gift is yours by God's choice, and not from "the spirit of the world"?_____

_____

Does the permanence of the gift give you an added level of responsibility for its use?_____ Why or why not?_____

_____

Ask God to give you a deeper understanding of His purpose for your life and of the areas of service in which your gifts can count the most for Him in the body of Christ.

Day 4 - Why Do Some Christians Never Discover Their Gift?
Scripture: James 4:2

How economical the Word of God is in proclaiming its profound truths! James 4:2 uses simple words that focus a bright light on a matter that seems to perplex the people of God. Why do many Christians never experience the blessings that God wants to give all of His children?

James cuts right to the heart of the problem. We do not **have** because we do not **ask**. He goes on in the next verse to explain that even when we do ask, we may not receive. There are good reasons. The asking requires a relationship with the one whom we ask. For many reasons, He will not respond to the self-seeking requests of His children. He is not responsive to a disobedient and willful child.

Can this be applied to the matter of discovering our spiritual gifts? Certainly. Many Christians never ask the Holy Spirit for help in discovering their gifts. Many really do not want to be involved in God's plan for world redemption. They are satisfied in their cozy comfort zones. Others don't know or don't believe that there is a gift to be received.

How can the church help those who are not aware of the gifts they are given?

_____

_____

Pray that your church will experience a new awareness of its responsibility in helping each member discover the spiritual gifts given by God for the common good.

Day 5 - Asking and Not Receiving
Scripture: James 4:3

Jesus told his disciples, "Ask, and it shall be given to you; seek, and you shall find; knock, and it shall be opened to you." (Luke 11:10) This is one of the great prayer promises of the Bible.

James has a different slant. In James 4:3 he writes:

You ask and do not receive, because you ask with wrong motives, so that you may spend it on your pleasures.

Is there a conflict? No, because the words of Jesus follow His teaching concerning perseverance in prayer by a righteous man. He teaches that His disciples should pray fervently seeking God's will. They are to place themselves in the midst of God's plan of serving other people.

But James is talking with people who pray in the midst of a sinful way of life and still expect God to respond as He would to those who are surrendered and faithful to Him. James says that we do not receive because our motives are wrong. We are only asking so we can have more of what we've already misused. We merely seek new levels of worldly enjoyment. He is saying that God will not honor that prayer.

Why do you want to discover your spiritual gift? Is it to boast about it to others? Or is it to offer that gift back to God for His service and blessing? What are your motives? How do you intend to use your gift once you have discovered it?

Write your thoughts here, then refer to them after lesson 6. _____
_____
_____

Ask God to reveal to you if your motive in seeking your spiritual gifts is acceptable to Him. Pray that anything self-centered might be removed so that the Holy Spirit can speak clearly to you and help you discover how your giftedness may be channeled into service.

Lesson 6

DISCOVERING YOUR SPIRITUAL GIFTS

Now we have received, not the spirit of the world, but the Spirit who is from God, that we might know the things freely given to us by God. 1 Corinthians 2:12

KEY THOUGHT

God distributes gifts according to His present activity in the world, and He wants us to discover them and use them to serve Him.

OUTLINE OF VIDEO LESSON

1. Four simple steps for discovering your spiritual gift:

    1) Discerning

    2) Surrendering/Empowering

    3) Developing

    4) Employing

2. Four assumptions necessary as we undertake this discovery process:

    1) You must be born again. Only believers can discern their spiritual gifts.

    2) You must trust the Holy Spirit to give good gifts.

    3) You must desire to know your gift.

    4) You must be willing to use your gift in service.

STEP 1: DISCERN

Six questions to ask yourself in the process of discernment: (1 Corinthians 2:9-12)

1. Have I _____ the Father in prayer what my gift is? (James 4:2-3)

2. What is the greatest _____ of my church?

3. What is my _____?

4. What gives me _____?

5. In what areas of ministry or service have others _____ me?

6. What areas of service have I _____?

1. The words "discover" and "discovery" are exciting words that usually always have a positive connotation. What are some discoveries you've made in recent years about yourself, your work, your relationships, or the Christian life that have been positive? List some and discuss them.

    _____

    _____

    _____

    _____

2. What role has prayer played in these experiences and to what extent? _____

    _____

    _____

    We can apply Romans 8:28 to the experiences of our lives and acknowledge that God is working all things together for _____, if we love Him and are called according to His _____. To discover life's choice spiritual treasures, we must consistently be trying to fit our lives into His plan and purpose.

3. If you could walk out of this study saying, "I have discovered my spiritual gift," what difference would you like it to make in your life? In other words, what would you want to see happen? Discuss.

    _____

    _____

4. We were reminded in the video lesson that a prerequisite to discovering our spiritual gifts is the experience of being _____ _____ into a personal relationship with Jesus Christ. Take a few moments to write out your understanding of what it means to be born again and to become a Christian.

    _____

    _____

    _____

    If you are not certain you have received Christ as your Savior and been born again, ask your facilitator or a staff member to assist you.

5. Discovery also involves asking ourselves serious questions and giving honest answers. In the video lesson we learned six questions to ask in the process of discernment.

    1) Have I _____ the Father in prayer what my gift is? How faithful and fervent have I been to pray?
    2) What is the greatest _____ of my church? What is the most urgent, critical, important need that touches my heart?
    3) What is my _____? Where do I feel intense conviction and burden? What challenges me or drives me?
    4) What gives me_____? What activities bring me satisfaction, inner peace, a sense of accomplishment?
    5) In what areas of ministry or service have others _____ me? Do people who know me and love me recognize my service as worthwhile and valuable?
    6) What areas of service have I _____? Have I been willing to help out and be of service whenever possible?

6. *Frank and Carol Graham* had been active in church for years. *Their faith in Christ ran deep. Yet in Frank's heart, a burden for full-time ministry continually surfaced and kept him searching. Try as he would, he could not escape the burden, so he decided to start going with a group of men to minister in prisons. He found great fulfillment in it.*

   The more he became involved in prison ministry, the greater his burden for full-time ministry became. He began training others and leading teams to testify and preach in prisons and train inmates in marriage and family issues. Eventually, he organized a non-profit ministry to help build free-standing chapel/training centers within prison walls.

   Frank's burden became a passion to help inmates bring about permanent change in their lives through Jesus Christ, so that once they got out of prison, they would never return. Prison ministry is now his full-time work. He says, "I believe my spiritual gift is 'bringing hope to life'."

   What do you think the steps were in Frank's discovery process? Discuss.

   _____

   _____

7. In your own heart, do you feel a longing -- a pull from within your spirit -- toward a cause or ministry area that could impact others and make a difference for the cause of Christ? Write it down, then share openly with the group. Commit to pray for one another.

   _____

   _____

   _____

8. Now look at the "Personal Assessment Guide" that follows. Notice that this is not a question and answer survey that you turn in to be evaluated or graded, but rather a dynamic tool designed to guide you through a personal conversation between God and yourself. In a sense, you will have an informal talk with God, examining your feelings and impressions from the Holy Spirit.

   While this experience is personal in nature, sharing your responses and conclusions with others in the group will be a positive and encouraging experience. Consider doing this during session 7.

PERSONAL APPLICATION

1. Write one thought or insight that God has impressed upon your heart during this lesson.

2. Identify at least one commitment you expect to make as a result of this lesson.

PERSONAL ASSESSMENT GUIDE

This guide is designed to help you think through your interests, abilities and spiritual gifts to gain insight into specific areas where the Lord may be leading you to serve or to continue serving. Please consider it a prayer guide. Prayer is always the key to discovering our spiritual gifts. Ask God to show you through this experience how He has ordered your heart and mind so you can enjoy a life of fulfilling service.

Complete the following statements and keep in mind that there are no right or wrong answers. The guide should be an honest reflection of your own thoughts. Please write in detail and be specific.

_____

When it comes to serving God through a ministry or area of church life, my experience has been_____.
I've been more of a _____ than a _____,
and the reason is _____.

Some areas of ministry I have been involved with in the past that brought me a great deal of satisfaction are _____
_____,
because _____.

Areas I've served in that seem to encourage others and where I received affirmation are
_____.

Some positions of responsibility I didn't feel comfortable with are _____
_____,
because_____.

Based on my training and background, I probably have more ability and expertise in the areas of _____.
What makes me successful in my work is _____.

When I'm with a group of people in a meeting or social gathering, I'm the type person who _____.
If people are there that I don't know, I _____.
If I'm in a meeting or planning session that calls for fresh ideas and fast action, I _____
_____.
If things are not well-organized and planned out, I _____,
to the extent that _____.

If I'm in a group that has the responsibility to make something happen, but direction and leadership seem to be lacking, I _____. And typically, I will _____.
In fact, if I'm given the choice of leading, following, or fitting somewhere in between, I prefer
_____.

I am deeply touched at different times by things I see or hear, through experiences with people, and by needs I hear about, such as_____
_____.
As I think about my church, I believe our greatest needs are_____
_____. The area or areas where I feel the strongest sense of burden or passion are_____

_____because_____.

When I think about Christ and what He has done for me, I feel _____
_____.
The Bible character or characters I identify with best are _____
_____, because _____
_____.

Some qualities and character traits I admire most in others and would like to characterize my own life are_____.

If I could have any real and lasting impact on people for the cause of Christ, I'd like it to be in the area of_____
because_____.

If I could be trained and really develop a strong confidence in a particular area of ministry, I'd want it to be_____.
The reason is _____.
If an opportunity for training were available, I would _____.

When my pastor, an associate, or someone else sounds an urgent call for help in a particular area, it's my nature to _____.

If you asked me to describe myself with words like "aggressive, laid back, quiet, loud, talkative, social, serious, organized, perceptive, driven, steady, reliable, results-oriented, loyal, encouraging, supportive, persuasive, regimented, a leader"...the words I'd choose to describe me are: _____
_____. I might even add a few others, such as _____
_____.
If my friends were to describe me, they would probably say I am _____
_____.

In summary -- and in terms of my overall abilities -- I'm probably best at _____
_____,
because _____.
People who know me best would say _____
_____.

As result of the biblical truths I have learned from this study, here are some some things I know for certain! I know that God created me, He loves me, and He has invested His very life in me. I know He wants me to live for Him and make a difference in the world with the one life I have. I know He wants me to touch as many people as I possibly can with the message of Christ, and I can do that best by serving Him through the church with the abilities and gifts He has given me.

I know I'm still in the process of becoming what God wants me to be, but I really believe He has hand-tailored me -- equipped me -- yes, <u>gifted</u> me -- to _____
_____.

I'm going to spend the rest of my life serving Him.

Signed_____ Date_____

DALE AND GERE DEAN HONEYCUTT, an Army colonel and his wife, joined the church on a Sunday morning and promptly told the pastor that they had already been assigned a job in the church.

They had visited the church the Sunday before and an associate pastor had told them of an area of urgent need. They thought that was great because they felt they had something to offer and were tired of not being used in the church where they currently belonged.

As the associate pastor got acquainted with Dale and Gere Dean, he found they were extremely intelligent, highly organized and self-motivated. Their background reflected dependability and consistency that said loud and clear: "Give us a job and we'll get it done no matter what! You can count on us!"

The job they were assigned was to follow up on the telephone with every person who made a decision for Christ and then get appropriate materials in their hands the very next week. They also scheduled new members for orientation, new Christians for baptism, verified personal information and kept on the lookout for potential new leaders.

When they had to be out of town, their responsibilities were always assumed by someone they had personally lined up. Their job was important to God, so it was important to them.

Dale and Gere Dean Honeycutt were a beautiful example of "serving God according to your giftedness." Success was always the result.

———————

Success in serving God is a reward for faithfulness in submitting our gifts and talents to Him, no matter where we are. When we discover our gifts and accept the fact that God wants us to use them in His plan, He provides the ways and means for us to develop and put our gifts to work.

The "Personal Assessment Guide" included as a key element of Lesson 6 provides a launching-pad for discovering and developing your spiritual gift. It is included in this study as a means of giving you insight into the activity of the Holy Spirit in your life. It will help prepare you to discover your gift and to discern how God wants you to translate the gift into a life of service.

Continue to work this week with your "Personal Assessment Guide." Let the daily Bible studies help to prepare you for your next lesson.

Lesson 7 brings a broader revelation of God's plan of giftedness. It includes more help in discovering your own gift. As you look forward to the final lessons of this study, remember the importance of a spiritual approach to this process. Discovering and using your spiritual gift is a significant part of your growth as a Christian.

The discovery of your spiritual gift is one of the most important pursuits of your life. Approach it prayerfully. God is eager to enrich your life with "the things freely given to us."

DAILY BIBLE STUDIES

Day 1 - We Have The Mind of Christ
Scripture: 1 Corinthians 2:16

Think of this: Your spiritual gift originated in the mind of God! It is His way of equipping you to be of real service to Him through your place in the body of Christ.

God has prepared good things for His children. He wants you to know what He has prepared for you. He wants to give it to you so your life may be fulfilled as well as committed to His redemptive purpose.

But how can you know what it is that God has prepared to give you? Paul says in 1 Corinthians 2:16 *"We have the mind of Christ."* It is impossible for us to know the full dimension of that statement. But one thing is certain: The mind of Christ brings all the power of the Holy Spirit into play in our lives to equip us to know the will of the Father and empower us to do it. The mind of Christ allows us to be surrendered to God's direction.

We have the mind of Christ. We must learn to use it. The Holy Spirit is our enabler.

Do you feel there is any hindrance in your gift discovery process? If so, what do you think it is?

_____

Ask the Holy Spirit to show you what it means to have the mind of Christ and how you can submit your will to His as a major step in using your spiritual gift. In the mean time, focus your attention on serving God. Discovery will follow.

Day 2 - Timothy: Discovery Leads to Development
Scripture: 1 Timothy 4:14-15

You will discover your spiritual gift through prayer and personal assessment. Perhaps you have already done so during this study. Once discovered, your gift must be developed. While these steps are still within the province of the Holy Spirit's provision, you also have a part to play. You have responsibility to cooperate with the Spirit. He will give power for focusing your will, your mind and body in the development of the gift. The result will be a life of service. Paul admonished Timothy:

Do not neglect the spiritual gift within you, which was bestowed upon you through prophetic utterance with the laying on of hands by the presbytery. Take pains with these things; be absorbed in them, so that your progress may be evident to all.
(1 Timothy 4:14-15)

Do you understand the "laying on of hands by the presbytery" spoken of by Paul to Timothy? It is equivalent to a more common practice of our day: the recognition by the church body of an individual who is surrendering his life and gifts to service.

Paul's real emphasis to Timothy is clear. Take pains. Be absorbed. The awareness and recognition of giftedness by the Christian is not to be taken lightly. We are to be serious about it. We are to focus attention on it. It is "for the common good," and should be "evident to all."

When you have discovered your gift, pray this prayer of commitment: Lord Jesus, I now make a commitment to devote my time and energies to the development of my gift and surrender it in service to you.

Day 3 - Timothy: Keep It Alive!

Scripture: 2 Timothy 1:6-7

The development and empowerment of the spiritual gift is a work of the Holy Spirit in the life of the believer. As you discover and contemplate your gift you will naturally ask certain questions. Why has God given it to me? How can it help me serve Him? What new responsibilities do I now assume?

The answers to these questions become more clear through your experiences at church and in your personal relationships. Recall Paul's advice to Timothy:

> *I remind you to kindle afresh the gift of God which is in you through the laying on of my hands. For God has not given us a spirit of timidity, but of power and love and discipline.* (2 Timothy 1:6-7)

Paul is saying to Timothy: "Keep the gift alive in you! Keep the fire lit under it. Don't let it grow ordinary or commonplace. God has given you the gift to enable you to be the person He wants you to be. Harness His power, love and discipline to activate your giftedness.

This is good advice for you as you meditate up on the gift of God in your life. It sets you apart from all other persons. It is unique and personal. Combined with your talents, personality, and life experiences, it equips you to serve Him.

What is your attitude about the gift you have been given and that you are now seeking to discover and develop?_____

As you move toward developing and exercising your gift, ask God to keep that flame of spiritual determination burning brightly in your heart.

Day 4 - Discovering What Comes Next

Scripture: Ephesians 4:14-16

During the first weeks of this study, we considered the lists of spiritual gifts contained in Romans 12, 1 Corinthians 12, and Ephesians 4. We have seen in the Romans and Corinthians passages that specific conclusions and definite results should be expected in the life of the one who has the gift and is developing and using it.

After revealing the true purpose of the spiritual gifts (Ephesians 4:12), Paul pictures the result to be expected when the entire body of Christ recognizes the gifts and exercises them as God intends:

> *As a result, we are no longer to be children, tossed here and there by waves, and carried about by every wind of doctrine, by the trickery of men, by craftiness in deceitful scheming; but speaking the truth in love, we are to grow up in all aspects into Him, who is the head, even Christ, from whom the whole body, being fitted and held together by that which every joint supplies, according to the proper working of each individual part, causes the growth of the body for the building up of itself in love.* (Ephesians 4:14-16)

Paul says that this comes from the maturing of the whole body (v. 13) through the ministry of gifts provided by the Father. We are to grow up. Together we become the body He can use for His eternal purpose.

Pray that you may see that kind of maturing in your church. Pray that your discovery and use of your spiritual gift will play a role in bringing it about!

Day 5 - The Source of Our Guidance
Scripture: Joshua 1:8

God told Joshua, "Moses my servant is dead." It was the end of a chapter in the life of the people of Israel. Moses was gifted by God for a purpose. He discovered his gift and used it as God led him.

But Moses was now dead and Joshua received the call to service. God told him what was expected of him (Joshua 1:2-9), and in the midst of the instructions God showed Joshua that there would be a vital step in his preparation -- a step that would guarantee success:

This book of the law shall not depart from your mouth, but you shall meditate on it day and night, so that you may be careful to do according to all that is written in it; for then you will make your way prosperous, and then you will have success. (Joshua 1:8)

Like Moses, Joshua was uniquely gifted by God for leading the people to their inheritance. As Paul would explain centuries later, those gifts were "for the common good." Moses, Joshua, Joseph, Nehemiah: all were gifted and led by the hand of God for a more far-reaching purpose than they ever imagined.

God tells Joshua that His Word will be the guide for his life and his leadership gift. The way for Joshua to find success was through meditation upon the Word and allowing it to be his guide in all that he did.

What do you think this might say to you concerning the use of your own gifts in service?_____

_____

Pray that you might find the Holy Spirit working in you in the same powerful way He worked in Moses, Joshua, Nehemiah, and other heroes of the faith.

Lesson 7

DEVELOPING YOUR SPIRITUAL GIFTS

...but speaking the truth in love, we are to grow up in all aspects into Him, who is the head, even Christ, from whom the whole body, being fitted and held together by that which every joint supplies, according to the proper working of each individual part, causes the growth of the body for the building up of itself in love.
Ephesians 4:15-16

KEY THOUGHT

You are the lever through whom the Holy Spirit applies the supernatural power of a sovereign God to human needs in the world today.

OUTLINE OF VIDEO LESSON

STEP 2 - SURRENDER/EMPOWER

1. The infilling of the Holy Spirit is not a once-for-all experience, but is a daily
    _____.

2. Words like "unction," "anointed," or "empowered" express what occurs when we
    _____ our gifts for ministry.

3. You can't be full of _____ and be full of the Spirit.

4. An acrostic for daily focus:

    M _____ upon the Lord and His Word.
    A _____ with God. ("I am yours. I have sinned. I am forgiven.")
    P _____ yourself as a living sacrifice. ("I give you my body and
                         my spiritual gifts.")
    S _____ Him joyfully!

STEP 3 - DEVELOP

Three ways to develop your spiritual gifts:

1. Through _____

2. Through _____

3. Through spiritual _____

1. Now that you have worked through the Personal Assessment Guide, take a few moments to reflect on it and write some of your observations in detail. Share with other members of the group some insights you have gained.

   _____

   _____

   _____

2. Notice the diversity of participants' backgrounds, interests, and gifts as reflected in the guide. Discuss the value -- the necessity -- of this diversity and how God uses it to bring balance in the life of the church.

   Do participants who are currently serving in places of responsibility feel that their gifts properly match their assignments? Share your responses.

3. Perhaps you have worked through the guide and still do not feel that you have discovered your spiritual gift. If so, that's all right. Remember, the major emphasis of our study is _____ God. Gift discovery follows willingness to serve.

   An excellent way to maintain daily focus for serving God is by using the acrostic M-A-P-S:

   M_____ upon the Lord and His Word.

   A_____ with God. ("I am yours. I have sinned. I am forgiven.")

   P_____ yourself as a living sacrifice. ("I give you my body and my spiritual gifts.")

   S_____ Him joyfully!

4. Most churches provide some type of training opportunities for their people to develop in areas of spiritual gifts and service. In the space below, identify some current needs or ministries and indicate the type of training opportunities that are available.

Current Needs/Ministries	_Training Currently Available_
_____	_____
_____	_____
_____	_____
_____	_____

5. Now discuss some needs, ministries, or areas of gift development for which you would like to see your church provide training. Offer some ideas for training, such as workshops, seminars, studies, etc. Keep your discussion positive. Be as specific as possible.

Areas of Need for Training and Gift Development	_Type of Training Needed_
_____	_____
_____	_____
_____	_____
_____	_____

6. The Ministry Opportunity Survey handed out by your facilitator is designed to acquaint you with some of the current needs in your church and how you can get involved in a place of service. The Personal Assessment Guide you have completed should have helped you gain insight into your spiritual giftedness. If you have questions about the survey, ask your facilitator for help.

Work through the Ministry Opportunity Survey at home, then bring it back with you to the next session.

PERSONAL APPLICATION

1. Write one thought or insight that God has impressed upon your heart during this lesson.

2. Identify at least one commitment you can expect to make as a result of this lesson.

LOOKING AHEAD
to the Next Lesson

GEORGE STOUT was a highly respected professor of music education at a major university where he was an innovator in the area of group keyboard instruction. He developed systems and materials that quickly established him as a pioneer in the field. Even with all his successes, one thing kept him from complete satisfaction in his career -- the lack of time for personal soulwinning. He maintained a busy pace at school, took care of his wife who had been in a wheelchair for years, and tried to lead as many people to Christ as he could.

His burden for unsaved people caused George to decide to take an early retirement. As soon as he was free from his school responsibilities, he showed up at the church ready to learn more about witnessing and pick up his assignments. He was determined to lead people to Christ. He learned several evangelism approaches and began leading soulwinning conferences and speaking for churches and conventions across America.

What made George effective as a trainer, however, was his consistency as a soulwinner himself. He never got his role as a witness and trainer confused. He kept the main thing primary: leading men and women to faith in Christ and training others to do the same.

When the challenge to serve God through evangelism reached George Stout's ears, he sensed the burden, responded to the call, got some training and got started. Armed with the confidence of God, he shared his faith wherever he went, leading people to Christ each week.

In his eighties now, George continues an active witness schedule today. To George, "It's all a matter of using what gifts and talents I have to serve God. That's what matters most."

Like George Stout, you can not only discover your spiritual gift, you can find ways of developing the gift. Start where you are. Look for training opportunities. Stay focused. You've already recognized the importance of discovering and developing your gifts. Now it's time to shift from the inward look of *What is my gift?* to the outward expression of *What do I do with my gift?*.

A key element in answering the *What do I do?* question is the "Ministry Opportunity Survey." Now you should be looking beyond the discovery process to the service areas where your gifts and abilities can best be applied. Remember these three things:

1. As a believer in Christ, you have been given at least one spiritual gift, perhaps more.
2. The purpose of your giftedness is to take your proper place of service within the body of Christ, for the building up of the body.
3. Your response is to apply your gifts and your life to the service of God.

The "Ministry Opportunity Survey" is an excellent tool to help you find a place of service. Be sure to complete it prayerfully and bring it with you for the next lesson.

As this study concludes with the next lesson, you will discuss some practical ways to serve the Lord according to God's design for your life. Prepare for that final lesson by devoting time each day to the Bible studies presented here. And commit yourself to a focus on MAPS every day!

DAILY BIBLE STUDIES

Day 1 - Putting It All Together
Scripture: Ephesians 4:7-16

As our study draws toward its close, we return to this scripture once more for a restatement of purpose. Paul says that the gifts are given "*...for the equipping of the saints for the work of service, to the building up of the body of Christ; until we all attain the unity of the faith, and of the knowledge of the Son of God, to a mature man, to the measure of the stature which belongs to the fullness of Christ...from (Christ) the whole body, being fitted and held together by that which every joint supplies, according to the proper working of each individual part, causes the growth of the body for the building up of itself in love.*"

Read this carefully again, for this is the "why" of spiritual gifts. Notice the key phrases: "*for the equipping of the saints for the work of service; building up of the body of Christ; attain the unity of the faith; fitted and held together by that which every joint supplies; the proper working of each part; growth of the body; building up of itself in love.*"

What is God's chosen instrument for impacting the world with the message of hope? The Church! And here Paul is talking about the mission of the church and the significant part each of us plays in it. By exercising our gifts and abilities we join in that great mission of making a difference in the world. What a thought!

Thank God for the chance you have to be a part of this dynamic mission.

Day 2 - The Price of Refusal
Scripture: Matthew 25:14-30

Jesus had much to say about what happens when we respond to Him. He spoke eloquently about the results of our decisions concerning His teaching.

In Matthew 25:14-30 Jesus shares keen insight into an inescapable truth. We are responsible for what we do with what we are given. In this parable He makes it clear that there are rewards for those who are faithful in using God's gifts. The alternative is a severe warning to those who are not faithful. Judgment awaits those who do not obey what Christ has shown to be His will and purpose.

We must apply this truth to the entire matter of service. God has promised blessing and reward for those who respond in faith and positive action. Good things happen when we take our place in the body of Christ (Ephesians 4:7-16). He has also demonstrated what can be expected by those who decide to ignore the truth He has shared.

You have learned many things during these seven weeks in *Serving God*. Write a key insight or two that you have gained. _____

_____

_____

Thank God for what you have learned and for your desire to obey Him.

Day 3 - The High Cost of Spiritual Astigmatism
Scripture: Numbers 13:1-33

You remember the story. Moses sent twelve spies across the river into the Promised Land with instructions to bring back a report on what they found. Each man was a leader representing one of the twelve tribes of Israel.

Something happened to ten of them on their way across the river. They developed a severe case of blurred spiritual vision. They took their eyes off the God who sent them and saw the land and its people through their own eyes of self-protection and self-absorption. So ten of the twelve came back with a report based on fear rather than on the certainty of God's provision and protection.

What happened? What always happens when we limit our spiritual vision with worldly logic and human reason. The ten spies forgot or ignored what God had already told them. God said "I will give you the land..." The land was theirs. They were not sent to make decisions concerning the possession of the land.

Have you ever been a deceptive spy when God called you to responsible activity? What in your opinion should have been the report of the spies? _____

_____

_____

The same lesson holds true for us as we cross the spiritual frontier where we seek God's will for our lives. His provision and promises are not up for discussion or evaluation. Our job is to obey and to respond. We are to follow the course He has outlined for us.

This is what *Serving God* is all about. Are you at the frontier? Have you crossed over the river? Having seen the other side are you now determining what your response must be?

Thank God for the reassurance He gives us when we are trusting and serving Him.

Day 4 - Timothy: Gifted and Committed
Scripture: Philippians 2:20-22

Paul, Timothy's mentor and spiritual father, spoke with respect and confidence about the young disciple: *"I have no one else like him, who takes a genuine interest in your welfare. For everyone looks out for his own interests, not those of Jesus Christ. But you know that Timothy has proved himself, because as a son with his father he has served with me in the work of the gospel."* (Philippians 2:20-22, NIV)

Timothy had demonstrated by his life of service at Paul's side that he was a man who could be trusted as overseer of the church at Philippi, a church that was especially dear to Paul's heart. What were the dynamics of this event?

Paul knew that the church needed a man who understood the gifts of God. Despite his youth, Timothy had endured failure and criticism. He had allowed himself to be shaped by God and by Paul into a "vessel fit for use" in God's plan. Timothy accepted the fact of his giftedness, prepared himself (1 Timothy 4:14-15), and allowed God to place him where his services were needed.

Timothy might have preferred to remain with Paul, but at God's command Paul and Timothy responded. Paul yielded his friend to God, and Timothy took on a task of great significance.

Ask God to help you capture the spirit of Timothy -- to be prepared and to respond with the dedication of your life when God reveals His plan for you.

Day 5 - Nehemiah: An Example for <u>You</u>
Scripture: Nehemiah 2:18

When they follow God's direction and serve according to their giftedness, God's people can accomplish impossible tasks. The story of Nehemiah is an example of a sovereign God giving supernatural power for a job that could not otherwise have been done.

Look at the sequence in Nehemiah's life. Through the witness of others God revealed a great need (1:1-3). The walls of Jerusalem had broken down. The city of God was defenseless, its gates burned. Nehemiah's first reaction was to weep and mourn, then to fast and pray (1:4). His prayer was one of confession on behalf of God's people (1:5-7) and a call upon God to remember His covenant with His people (1:8-11).

God had already given Nehemiah great gifts, but they had not yet been used in service. Nehemiah had been given a position of high responsibility as cupbearer to the king of Babylon (1:11). He had gifts of administration and leadership. Now God called on him to use those gifts in a life of service to the one who created him and on behalf of the people of God.

Nehemiah responded in faith and obedience. God paved the way. He opened the heart of the king to allow Nehemiah to go back to Jerusalem and to give him support of every kind. Nehemiah led the rebuilding of the walls in 52 days! An impossible task? Yes, except that here is a man gifted and empowered by God, and willing to be used. He surrendered his gifts to God for the common good. The result was the accomplishing of what only God could have done.

Does the life and work of Nehemiah fit the pattern set out by Paul in his description of the gifts of God and their use in Romans, 1 Corinthians, and Ephesians? How is God's dealing with His people throughout history -- in both Old Testament and New Testament times -- different from the way he deals with His people today?_____

_____

_____

Ask God to make you sensitive to every opportunity of service when you hear about it, so that when called upon, you'll be ready.

Lesson 8

SERVING GOD!
MAKING A DIFFERENCE!

His master replied, "Well done, good and faithful servant! You have been faithful with a few things; I will put you in charge of many things. Come and share your master's happiness!" Matthew 25:21 (NIV)

KEY THOUGHT

You are gifted to serve God. What you are doing now with your life can touch the world and impact eternity.

OUTLINE OF VIDEO LESSON

STEP 4 - EMPLOY

1. Five things you will *miss* if you fail to discover and employ your spiritual gifts:

   • The discovery of your created purpose.
   • The joy of becoming what you were _____ to be.
   • The triumph over mediocrity by the realization of your God-given potential.
   • Absolute fulfillment of serving alongside the Creator in His redemptive plan.
   • The unparalleled _____ of effectively ministering to others.

2. Four things you will *experience* if you choose to discover and employ your spiritual gifts:

   • You can make a difference in your family, your community, and your church.
   • You can literally make a difference in the _____!
   • You can touch the world and impact eternity.
   • One day you will hear the words, "_____ _____, good and faithful servant."

3. Three principles in using your gifts:

   • Gifts are employed to serve _____.
   • Gifts are employed for the ministry of the _____.
   • Gifts are employed under the authority of the local _____.

The church will impact eternity, so your gifts, your time, and your resources can only be invested for eternity through the Church. That's why God gifted you! That's why He empowered you!

CONFESSION

I, _____,
*am created in the image of God, redeemed by the grace of God,
filled and gifted by the Spirit of God, and chosen by the hand
of God to serve alongside Him for the redemption of the world.
I will serve God joyfully for the rest of my life!*

---

1. The key question in your mind at this point in our study may be, "Now what?" "What do I do next? What does God expect of me?" What do you think God does expect of you? Make some notes and share with the group.

   _____

   _____

   _____

   Do you honestly believe you can accomplish what God expects of you? _____

2. Remember the story of Joshua, Caleb, and the spies in Numbers 13-14? The attitude of the spies was _____!

   In contrast, Joshua and Caleb's response in Numbers 14:9 was _____

   _____

3. When called upon to take a place of responsibility in the church, people sometimes say, "I can't do that. I'm too insignificant. I couldn't make any difference anyway."

   As result of God's speaking to us during this study, what do you feel our attitude toward opportunities for service should be?

   _____

4. By now you have worked through the Ministry Opportunity Survey and brought it to the session ready to give to your facilitator. Before turning the survey in, review together:

   - The current needs of your church
   - The response of participants to these needs through the survey
   - Areas of special background and training
   - Areas where participants would like to receive training
   - Additional ministry ideas and thoughts suggested by participants
   - The response of participants who are ready to serve now

5. We were reminded in a previous lesson to keep our eyes focused on the _____ of gifts, not on the gifts themselves. The main goal of our study is to discover who _____ is, to get to know Him. Discovering our gifts will follow.

6. Ephesians 4:1-16 teaches us that God does have a plan and purpose for our lives. We are integral members of a body of believers who are chosen by God to serve together to _____ up the church. God's plan is for us to grow and mature in our _____ in Him, and to recognize Christ as the _____ of the body. The end result of our carrying out God's purpose for our lives is the growth of the _____ so it can be built up in love.

7. We have come to understand that Paul's lists of gifts in 1 Corinthians, Romans, and Ephesians should not be understood as comprehensive, but rather as _____ or illustrative. God always gifts His church to do what He has _____ it to do in any generation. And the number of gifts is dependent upon the need of the church and the sovereign work of the _____ _____. God will give a church the _____ mix needed to accomplish its purpose.

8. In trying to discover our spiritual gift, we need to ask "What is my _____ for seeking my gift?" That motive should be "...for the _____ of the church." 1 Corinthians 14:12

9. We have learned the significance of _____ in discovering our spiritual gifts. (James 4:2-3) Filling our personal assessment guides and surveys will not reveal to us what we can receive only from the Holy Spirit in prayer. Guides and surveys follow prayer.

10. We have learned that we develop our spiritual gifts:

   • Through _____
   • Through _____
   • Through _____ _____

11. In closing this study, we are actually beginning a lifelong journey of significance and fulfillment that comes from serving God. Completing the study, attending every session, and doing all the daily Bible studies -- as important as these are -- are not enough!

   Serving God comes down to a matter of personal choice and willingness. You must exercise your will. What matters most to God is not how much you know, but what you are willing to <u>do</u> with what you know.

   Do not let a single day go by without following your MAPS !

   • M_____ upon the Lord and His Word.
   • A_____ with God that you are forgiven and that you belong to Him.
   • P_____ yourself to God each day as a living sacrifice.
   • S_____ Him joyfully!

13. Repeat the confession together.

CONFESSION

I, _____,
am created in the image of God, redeemed by
the grace of God, filled and gifted by the Spirit of God,
and chosen by the hand of God to serve
alongside Him for the redemption of the world.
I will serve God joyfully for the rest of my life!

You can do it. In His strength, just go ahead and <u>do</u> it!
Serve God! And make a difference in the world!